I am JEWISH!

WRITTEN BY
SHARI LAST

Shalom! I am Jewish and my favourite colour is orange.

I am Jewish and I travel the world with my family.

I am Jewish and my grandma tells me stories about when she was younger.

I am Jewish and I don't know any other Jewish kids.

I am Jewish and I pray every day.

We are Jewish and we love watching TV!

I am Jewish and my favourite sport is basketball.

I am Jewish but my cousins are not.

I am Jewish like my mum.

I am Jewish and I light Shabbat candles every week.

I am Jewish and I want to be famous!

There is no ONE way to be Jewish.
There is no one way to be ANYTHING!

How would you describe yourself?

I am _____

I am _____

I am _____

Write down three things that make you YOU!

1.	2.	3.

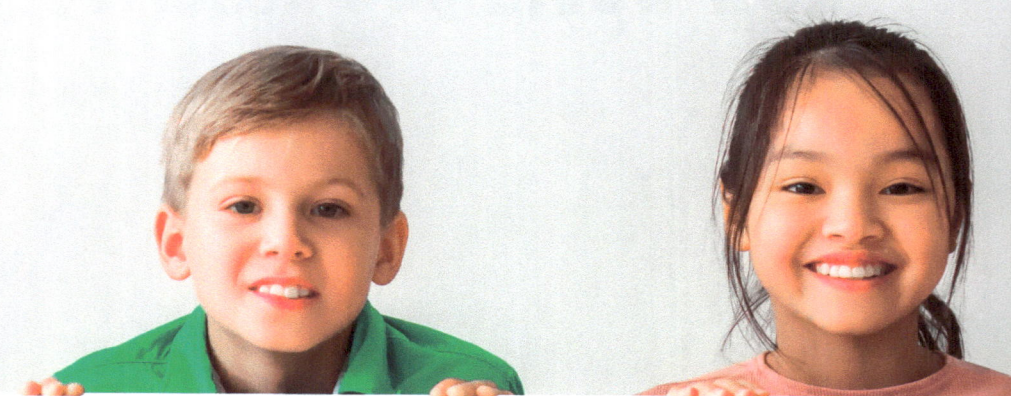

First published in Great Britain in 2024
Cupcake Press,
an imprint of
TELL ME MORE Books

Text copyright ©2024 Shari Last
Design copyright ©2024 Shari Last

ISBN: 978-1-917200-11-0

Picture credits: Thanks to Adobe Stock.

All rights reserved. Without limiting the rights under the copyright reserved above, no part of this publication may be reproduced, stored in, or introduced into a retrieval system, or transmitted, in any form, or by any means (electronic, mechanical, photocopying, recording or otherwise), without the prior written permission of the copyright owner.

CUPCAKE PRESS

Tell Me More!
NEW IDEAS FOR KIDS

Visit our website:
www.tellmemorebooks.com

www.ingramcontent.com/pod-product-compliance
Lightning Source LLC
Chambersburg PA
CBHW050749110526
44591CB00002B/26